Feeling Guilty?

Grace for Your Mistakes

Steve Brown

New Growth Press, Greensboro, NC 27404
www.newgrowthpress.com
Copyright © 2016 by Key Life

All rights reserved. No part of this publication may be reproduced, stored in a retrieval system, or transmitted in any form by any means, electronic, mechanical, photocopy, recording, or otherwise, without the prior permission of the publisher, except as provided by USA copyright law.

Unless otherwise indicated, all Scripture quotations are taken from the *Holy Bible, English Standard Version*®. Copyright © 2000; 2001 by Crossway Bibles, a division of Good News Publishers. Used by permission. All rights reserved.

Scripture verses marked NIV are taken from the Holy Bible, New International Version ®, Copyright © 1973, 1978, 1984 by the International Bible Society. Used by permission of Zondervan. All rights reserved.

Cover Design: Tandem Creative, Tom Temple, tandemcreative.net

Typesetting: Lisa Parnell, lparnell.com

ISBN: 978-1-942572-33-6 (Print)
ISBN: 978-1-942572-34-3 (eBook)

Library of Congress Cataloging-in-Publication Data
 Names: Brown, Stephen W., author.
 Title: Feeling guilty? : grace for your mistakes / Steve Brown.
 Description: Greensboro, NC : New Growth Press, 2016.
 Identifiers: LCCN 2015040553 | ISBN 9781942572336 (print) | ISBN 9781942572343 (ebook)
 Subjects: LCSH: Guilt—Religious aspects—Christianity. | Grace (Theology) | Forgiveness of sin.
 Classification: LCC BT722 .B76 2016 | DDC 234—dc23
 LC record available at http://lccn.loc.gov/2015040553

Printed in China

23 22 21 20 19 18 17 16   1 2 3 4 5

The other day my assistant Cathy told me that there was a man on the phone who urgently needed to talk to me. Cathy was laughing. "He says that he's a very big fan, but he's lying because he called you Dr. Green."

So I picked up the phone and said hello. "With whom am I'm speaking?" I asked. The man said that he would rather not tell me his name because he was going to tell me some really bad things he had done and was feeling too embarrassed and guilty to tell me his name. "Okay, I'm going to call you 'Sam.'" There followed a conversation between two sinners who didn't know each other's names. He confessed, and I responded with "So?"

"What do you mean 'So?'"

"You thought that you surprised God and he had such high hopes for you? You really think that Christ died for everybody's sins but yours? Do you think that Christ died for only small stuff like white lies and not flossing?"

Then I told him what I'm going to tell you. People often ask me why I talk so much about sin. To be honest with you, it is because I'm such a great sinner. I understand guilt. I don't like guilt, but I've faced it and dealt with it.

And God is a great God who loves me even though he knows me in ways you will never know me. That is true of you too. As Christians, we need to go back to the basics of the faith. We forget that Jesus hung on a cross, dying for desperate people—winos, prostitutes, thieves, and other hopeless sinners. Christ came to people who couldn't make it on their own.

Most people feel guilty, including me and you. That's bad? No, that's good. One of the problems of living in this world is that they have lied to us about everything. That which seems good really isn't, and that which seems bad really is. Guilt is a proper, good, and mighty instrument in the hand of the God of the universe.

The truth is that we are guilty. The problem is that we don't understand the solution. Obedience grows in us through the grace and freedom of the gospel. Not the other way around. Keep reading to find out why guilt is a good thing and what to do when you notice you are guilty. You will find that guilt is not your enemy, but that, rightly handled, it can be the beginning of a life of freedom.

What Good Is Guilt?

Psalm 32 is a comparison between those who are redeemed and those who aren't, not between the good and the bad. The question we face is, *What good is guilt?*

Guilt hurts (and that's a good thing)

> For when I kept silent, my bones wasted
> away
> through my groaning all day long.
> For day and night your hand was heavy
> upon me;
> my strength was dried up as by the
> heat of summer. *Selah*
> (Psalm 32:3–4)

I remember looking out over a leper colony from where I spoke in Taiwan. The sight of their hands, feet, ears, and faces eaten away was horrible. In talking with the doctors, I discovered the problem with leprosy isn't the disease itself; the problem is that it takes away pain. For example, if they put their hand on a hot stove, they don't know it is a problem. Because it doesn't hurt, they don't move their hand. Without the help of pain to keep them safe, someone with leprosy will slowly lose parts of their body.

Guilt is meant to work a bit like physical pain, but in the spiritual realm. Guilt hurts, and it hurts really bad. Guilt tells you to move away from thoughts and behaviors that are bad for you or others, and it is a gift from God to keep your soul safe. The conviction of God's Spirit in the life of the believer (part of the job description of the

Holy Spirit) is sometimes painful. But the upside is that it lets you know you are spiritually alive. Does it sometimes hurt because you were disobedient? That is okay. It is a sign that there is still hope for change in you.

But, even if you don't change, the guilt is the reminder that God cares. There is nothing worse than a parent who never cares enough to correct. Guilt is the price you pay for desires, thoughts, words, and deeds that are against God's good will for you (and of course there are usually other prices to be paid too). But isn't there comfort in knowing that you worship a God who cares deeply about you and about what you do?

I met a thirty-two-year-old woman once who had been a prostitute. She heard about Jesus and how he accepted prostitutes so she came to me and asked if I would help her. She talked about her life on drugs and how, in order to pay for the habit, she had to sell herself. As the woman poured out her story, she began to cry. She reached into her purse, pulled out a rumpled photograph, and threw it across my desk. The photograph was of a little girl. She said, "That was me when I was three years old. Sometimes, after I've turned a trick, when I'm high and trying to sleep, I'll pull that picture out, look at that little girl, and say, 'My God, what have I done to you?'"

Her life had gone in directions she never intended. She was from a nice family and had even been brought up in the church. But one thing led to another and one day she realized that she had violated God's plan for her life. Now she didn't even feel like she could pray—she believed that God was angry and condemning and that she was beyond his forgiveness. The reality of sin and guilt hurt deeply.

Contrary to what many in our culture would say, sin is real and feeling guilty is a genuine and honest reaction to the sin. It's not just your issues, the way you were potty trained or how hard it was to please your father—those things sometimes are in play in "false" guilt. But, aside from that, real sin (and we are *real* sinners) brings real guilt.

The Bible says, "The heart is deceitful above all things, and desperately sick; who can understand it?" (Jeremiah 17:9). If you really believe that, why are you so shocked by your own sin? And the Bible says, "If we say we have no sin, we deceive ourselves, and the truth is not in us" (1 John 1:8). Again, if you really believe that, why are you so shocked by your own sin?

There are four steps in the process of guilt. First, we do something bad. Second, we feel guilty. Third, we get punished. Fourth, after the punishment, we are free of the guilt. There is something psychologically healthy about punishment that releases you from guilt. This may sound strange to you since we don't often talk about punishment nowadays, but when we talk about punishment here, what we're really talking about is the repayment of a debt you owe because of what you've done. If you break a window, your punishment is to pay the cost of replacement. Repayment becomes more complicated when we do injury to God or others or even ourselves.

This is where we start to get overwhelmed, when we see that our debts cannot easily be repaid. It hurts to really see how we have hurt God and others. It hurts to realize that there are real and painful consequences for our actions. Many people spend their lives trying to avoid responsibility for their actions. They run from the pain of punishment, but cannot escape the pain of guilt, whether in their consciences or in the consequences of their actions.

On the other hand—and this is important—if there is no first step, there will be no fourth step. In other words, if you haven't done anything bad to which you can attach the guilt you feel, but still feel guilty, your natural inclination is to get punished and thereby attempt to be free. This is false guilt. That effort to be punished will only make you feel more guilty. Then you will only punish yourself more and, as a result, feel even more guilty. It is a vicious cycle. That is why a lot of people fail. They are accepting the punishment they think is their due. Either way, it hurts.

Guilt doesn't take place in a vacuum. It is always in the context of what God has revealed in the law and in the entirety of Scripture. When we have "real" guilt, it is always because we have measured our lives by what God says. Real guilt is the compass God uses to lead us back to Christ where we can be reminded that he has paid the debt for *all* our sins. There is no more punishment left for us. We are forgiven, and if we're forgiven there's no reason to be swallowed up by guilt.

There's also no need to avoid or be afraid of guilt that leads you to forgiveness. If we stray from the road to home, there is always real guilt, honest confession and repentance, and an effort to once again head for home. Praise God for your guilt. That compass is one of the most valuable gifts God has given his own.

Guilt motivates

> I acknowledged my sin to you,
>   and I did not cover my iniquity;
> I said, "I will confess my transgressions to
>   the LORD,"
>   and you forgave the iniquity of my
>   sin. (Psalm 32:5)

Feeling Guilty?

A psychologist friend of mine says that the only purpose for guilt is to send you to God for forgiveness. Once that is accomplished, it has no purpose. Guilt motivates, but let me tell you, it also manipulates.

The problem with what goes on in religious circles is that we have learned how to manipulate people with guilt. We sometimes do that with good motives, but often it is a way to acquire power or to build empires for self. In our "Born Free" seminars I demonstrate how that works. First I tell the people in the seminar the following story:

> Alexander the Great had a judgment day for cowardice on the battlefield every Thursday. One day, while Alexander sat on his judgment throne, a young man was brought to him. Those who were there said that for the first time, they saw a softening on the face of Alexander. As he looked at the young man, perhaps he thought of the young man's girlfriend back home, of the children to come from their marriage, of the parents who loved him. Alexander the Great looked at the young man and asked, "What is your name?" The young man said, "Ale . . . Alex . . . Alexander, sir." The softness went from Alexander the Great's face. He jumped up from his throne, walked down the steps, picked up

the young man and threw him in the dirt. He said, "Young man, change your name or change your ways."

That's the story, and then in a serious and sober, no-nonsense way, I say, "When is the last time you led someone to Christ? How much time did you spend in God's Word this morning? Have you really prayed or only nodded in God's direction? Do you tithe? If you are affluent and you only tithe, you're robbing God. How much more do you give? Do you . . ."

I keep asking painful guilt-producing questions until I can't do it any longer without laughing. The Key Life staff bets among themselves on how far I can go without losing it. But you should see the people sitting in front of me and the extreme discomfort they show on their faces.

Then I say, "I just manipulated you with guilt. What you're feeling right now is how the manipulators get you to do what they want you to do, and they usually want more from you than you can give."

Guilt can motivate you to the throne, but it can also manipulate you into doing what others want you to do. Because you're free and forgiven, you should never be manipulated. It is a sin to manipulate, but it is also a sin to be manipulated. You belong to no one but God. You should be obedient to no one but him. He is the One who, through his Spirit, convicts of sin, points to Jesus, and draws us to the throne.

There is a difference between the manipulation that others use to get us to do what they want and the conviction of the Holy Spirit who moves in us. One is harsh and the other is gentle; one is broad and the other is specific. One is often not fixable, while the other is doable.

I have a friend I hurt the day before yesterday. He's a good friend, and we've walked together for a long time. I didn't even know I had hurt him . . . and certainly not as deeply as I did. The next morning in prayer when I brought his name before the throne of God, something in me turned dark. In a flash I remembered what I had said and how I had said it. I figuratively "left my gift on the altar" and picked up the phone and called my friend and asked for his forgiveness. He, of course, forgave me. In fact, we cried together on the phone. When I went back to my prayers, I was drawn to the throne and sensed the pleasure of God. I can't tell you how many times the Holy Spirit, with gentleness but also with clarity, reminds me of my sin. He uses the Scripture, sometimes a preacher, and sometimes a brother or sister. The Holy Spirit uses conviction to motivate me to ask God and others for forgiveness. The Holy Spirit reminds me that in Christ I can be assured of God's forgiveness and love no matter what. When I'm sensitive, I'm thankful for guilt.

Guilt defines

> Therefore let everyone who is godly
>   offer prayer to you at a time when
>   you may be found;
> surely in the rush of great waters,
>   they shall not reach him. . . .
> Many are the sorrows of the wicked,
>   but steadfast love surrounds the one
>   who trusts in the LORD.
>   (Psalm 32:6, 10)

How can you be godly and a sinner at the same time? Martin Luther called that *Simul Justus et Peccator,* and it means that we are righteous and a sinner at the same time. We have defined godliness in terms of purity when godliness should be defined in terms of repentance. The fact is, we don't even know what repentance means. Cleaning up spilt milk is not repentance; cleaning it up is the result of repentance.

One of the Old Testament words for repentance means "to comfort." The New Testament word means something that has gone on in your mind that eventually manifests itself in your life.

Repentance is when you look to the God of the universe and know who you are and who he is, and what you have done and what needs to be changed. That's all. It is not changing. It is God's methodology of change if he sees fit to change us, and he usually does. If repentance meant changing, I could never repent. There are things in my life that I simply can't change. God knows it, and I know it. Radical and pervasive depravity is a part of my life on this earth. Repentance is, in effect, agreeing with God that there is no hope for us without Jesus.

One time when I was a pastor, a young leader in the youth ministry came into my study. I was reading a book and looked up. Sarah said, "I went to a Bible study last night and I learned some really good stuff. I learned that you can't hug a stiff kid." I said to her, "That's a good illustration. I'll use it sometime." Then I went back to my reading, hoping she would leave. She just stood there. Finally, I asked, "What is it, Sarah?" She said, "I learned something else last night. I went to babysit after the Bible study for a two-year-old. He had played in the mud all day and was the dirtiest kid I have ever seen. I walked into his room and he lifted up his arms to be hugged. I found out that it's easier to hug a dirty kid than it is to hug a stiff kid." So true.

I'm not worried about your dirt. Jesus already took care of that on the cross. When Jesus said "It is finished," it really was. He took your sin to the cross. And not only that, Paul talks a lot about what theologians call *imputation*. That means that he took your sin and gave you the goodness, the obedience, the perfection of Christ. Whenever you stand before God, you are clothed in the righteousness of Christ. Your sin is covered, but the stiffness (e.g., "I'll do it my way," "I am my own master," "I'll control this situation, thank you") will kill you.

When you read Matthew 23 where Jesus said so many harsh things about the religious leaders—and they were the most genuinely righteous people around—he spoke to their stiffness. And not only that, the reason Jesus hung out with the prostitutes, the drunks, and the sinners (so much so that he was called one) was because he had trouble dealing with the stiffness of the good people. Sometimes God brings obedience and sanctification (obedience being harder and sanctification longer than most suppose), and he can do that more easily when stiffness isn't the problem.

Guilt discovers

You are a hiding place for me;
> you preserve me from trouble;
you surround me with shouts of deliverance.
(Psalm 32:7)

It's always a surprise to go to God, expecting to be struck down by a lightning bolt, only to find out that you're hugged instead. The principle is this: love in response to goodness is not love; it is reward. I have wonderful daughters, but when they were growing up they weren't perfect. If they had been, they would never have known my love for them. If they had been perfect, they would have thought that I was rewarding them for their obedience. It was only in the context of that which was not lovable that I was able to demonstrate my love.

Sometimes the most religious people seem to have the hardest time understanding that God is not a policeman; he is your father (Matthew 7:11). My father was a drunk and did a lot of bad things, but he loved me. Whenever I think of the love of God, I think of the love of my father, multiplied a hundred million times. My guilt forces me to the throne so that a big God might reach out and hold me in the midst of my dirt, thankful that I'm no longer stiff.

But there is more to the "discovery" than that. The things that make us feel guilty (the violation of the ways God would have us live that are reflected in the Bible) is a discovery of a very wise way to live. Christians, because God has revealed it to us, know how the world works, what will make for a better life, and how to be as happy as one can be in a fallen world. That's the law he has given us and the law, which any respectable Jewish rabbi would agree, is a great gift from God.

The law was not given to ruin our lives, to make us miserable, or to forbid that we enjoy. To the contrary, the law is a gift revealing where the mines in the minefields are. So those areas where you feel guilty are, in fact, the areas where you're hurting yourself. In that sense, guilt is God saying to us, "Child, let me show you a better way to do this."

Guilt corrects

> I will instruct you and teach you in the
>   way you should go;
>   I will counsel you with my eye upon
>   you.
> Be not like a horse or a mule, without
>   understanding,
>   which must be curbed with bit and
>   bridle,
>   or it will not stay near you.
> (Psalm 32:8–9)

Do you know why I'm obedient? Do you know why the law is there? Because I want to please God. The only way I know what pleases God is from the Scripture and from the law, both a reflection of the God of the universe who loves me even if I never obey one of the laws.

Are you faithful because God will really get you if you're not? He won't, you know. He loves you. But he does plan to break through your stiffness.

Paul said, "We are constrained by the love of Christ" (2 Corinthians 5:14, author paraphrase). The reason your besetting sin is so besetting is so you might go to God and allow him to love you. Your response is constrained (or limited) by that kind of unconditional acceptance, making you much more likely to respond with love and obedience.

Guilt brings joy

> Be glad in the LORD, and rejoice, O righteous,
> and shout for joy, all you upright in heart! (Psalm 32:11)

Guilt, when it's removed, brings great joy. That is why Christians can walk around with such a silly grin on our faces. We are forgiven.

Joy isn't something you work at. Joy comes when you know who you are and what needs to be changed. It is the realization that God is going to love you, even if you never change. Joy is what happens when you're forgiven.

Don't worry about holiness; it will follow. Don't worry about obedience; that is the Holy Spirit's business. The God of the universe forgives you without a kicker. You can laugh—*really* laugh—because you are free and forgiven.

Forgiven and Forgotten

Right now you may be feeling guilty about one thing or another: what you said to your spouse last night, those unrelenting thoughts, something you did years ago and regret, actual lying and cheating, the places where you struggle right now. What do you do with this guilt? Do you try to ignore it? Bury it? Would you like to know how to handle it for good, how to find true and lasting forgiveness?

Let me give you an important principle for believers: *definition is a prerequisite to recovery*. In other words, if you can define a problem, you can usually deal with it. Vague anxiety without definition of its source will simply wipe you out. It's important to define the problem before you do anything else. Let's define forgiveness based on Hebrews 10:1–18. Is true forgiveness even possible?

The requirement for forgiveness

To receive forgiveness, we must be sanctified, which simply means "set apart" to God. A lot of people try to make Christian principles work before they become Christians. When Jesus spoke to his disciples, one provision always followed upon the heels of his counsel: you must be a disciple of Jesus in order to reap the benefits of discipleship.

When Jesus said, "My peace I give to you," "These things I have spoken to you, that my joy may be in you," "Though he die, yet shall he live," or "I am with you always," he was only talking to a certain kind of person. Those are not universal statements applicable to everyone; they are meant only for his everlasting family. So a word of caution: forgiveness is only for those who have gone to the only One who can forgive, Jesus Christ.

The reality of forgiveness

The forgiveness Christ offers is the real thing; it's not a mere shadow or a copy. Let me illustrate what I mean. If I am really thirsty, one of the most arresting pictures I can see is a picture of a glass of cold water. The picture may be beautiful, it may make me think or daydream about a glass of water, but it is not a real glass of cold water. No matter how nice or realistic the picture, it is just that, a picture. In the same way, Christ's forgiveness really makes you clean and free. You are forgiven. That is reality.

The result of forgiveness

Forgiveness doesn't come cheap. It never has and it never will. If I punch you in the nose and you decide to forgive me, that forgiveness costs something—a hurting, damaged nose. There's a sense in which all forgiveness is vicarious, substitutionary, one for another. Forgiveness always costs somebody something. In the case of the forgiveness offered by God, it cost him his Son. Christ took your place. His death means that you don't have to die. Remember the cost.

The reliability of forgiveness

"But when Christ had offered for all time a single sacrifice for sins, he sat down at the right hand of God" (Hebrews 10:12). Forgiveness is a fact because the One in authority, Jesus Christ, says it is a fact. No data, no situation, no tragedy, no governmental decree, no military effort, nothing can ever change it.

There was once a doctor in a mining town with many patients who simply couldn't pay their bills. When they couldn't pay, the doctor wrote "Canceled" beside their debts in his books. Years later, when the physician died, his widow tried to collect on those debts by taking the past debtors to court. But the court replied, "If your husband said that their debt is canceled, it is canceled and can never be claimed again." Likewise, the King who rules has declared you "Forgiven." And no one can change that fact.

The reach of forgiveness

The reach of forgiveness is vast, "once for all" (Hebrews 10:10). Jesus forgave every sin you have ever committed, every sin you are committing, and every sin you will ever commit. How about that? Corrie ten Boom described it like this, "Jesus takes your sin, past, present and future, dumps it in the ocean and puts up a sign that reads 'No Fishing.'" That is so true. Christ has given forgiveness as far into the future as our lives will reach. And he has given forgiveness into the past as far back as our lives have been lived. We really are free.

I know what you're thinking: *Well, does that mean I can do anything I want and I'm already forgiven?* Yes, that's what it means. *In that case, I'm going out right now to really sin since it's forgiven anyway.* You may do that, but if you do, you haven't understood the motivation of love. I don't try to be obedient because he will zap me if I'm not. I try to be obedient because he loved me when I wasn't. I'm constrained by his love, not by his judgment.

The reminder of forgiveness

In Hebrews 10:17 God says, "I will remember their sins and their lawless deeds no more."

There was a bishop who was a confessor for a nun. One day the nun told him that Christ had revealed himself to her in person. The bishop, understandably doubtful about her vision, said to her, "I have some instructions for you. The next time Christ appears to you, I want you to ask him about the sins of the archbishop." The nun said,

"Of course." So the next time, in a period of confession, the bishop said to the nun, "Well, did you ask Christ about the sins of the archbishop?" She said, "Yes, I did." He replied, "What did he say?" The nun answered, "He said, 'I've forgotten.'"

The living sacrifice of Jesus Christ has not only wiped your slate clean, it has broken your slate into a million pieces across crossbeams. "There is therefore now no condemnation for those who are in Christ Jesus" (Romans 8:1). God has forgiven your sin on the cross. Christ's death reminds us.

You may be on a guilt trip. I want you to think for a moment about the most horrible sin you have ever committed. Think about that which, if I revealed it to your friends and family, would make you want to crawl into a hole in the ground. It may be a sin you've hidden for years, the one thing that nobody knows and about which you're never going to tell anyone because you're so ashamed.

Now hold it, in all of its blackness, before the light of Christ. Remember God's Word in Hebrews 10. He says this to you: "You remember your forgiveness, and I'll forget your sin. You are free!" That's real. That's secure. That's yours—forever. That is the gateway and the path of real life now and real life forever. Welcome to the world of the forgiven!

Are you tired of "do more, try harder" religion?

Key Life has only one message, to communicate the radical grace of God to sinners and sufferers. Because of what Jesus has done, God's not mad at you.

On radio, in print, on CDs and online, we're proclaiming the scandalous reality of Jesus' good news of radical grace…leading to radical freedom, infectious joy and surprising faithfulness to Christ.

For all things grace, visit us at **KeyLife.org**